Warren Buffett

The Life, Lessons & Rules For Success

Influential Individuals

Table of Contents

Introduction

He's been consistently voted one of the wealthiest people *in the world.* Time Magazine also voted him as one of the most influential people in the world; widely considered to be the most successful investor of the entire 20th century.

In short, Warren Buffett is a boss.

The man knows a thing or two about success. With a net worth of $77.1 billion, the billionaire investor's fabled business acumen has inspired everything from investment books to college courses. He is known to favor long-term investment strategies, like dollar cost averaging, which encourages the regular purchase of the same investment over time. He also has long-standing holdings in the Coca-Cola Company, Apple, and American Express among others. His now infamous letters to Berkshire Hathaway shareholders help shed light into how the man they call the "Oracle of Omaha," reads the tealeaves.

This book takes a look at Buffett's life. From humble beginnings in Omaha, up to present day where the 86 year old is still going strong. We take a look at his first taste of business at the ripe old age of 6, following on with his major successes and failures along the way. The aim of this book is to be educational and inspirational with actionable principles you can incorporate into your own life straight from the great man himself.

Early Life

"I always knew I was going to be rich. I don't think I ever doubted it for a minute."

Warren Buffett is one of the most prominent investors of the past two generations. His philanthropy activities have caught the eye worldwide, and this past March he was considered the second wealthiest individual in the United States.

Buffett was born in 1930 in Omaha, Nebraska, and has two siblings. His father was a Congressman who had high hopes that his son would one day go into politics just like he did. However, Buffett saw a different track for his life from a very early age, whether his father liked it or not. Attending Rose Hill Elementary School, his father sought election to the United States Congress, and this uprooted the entire family to Washington, D.C. where Buffett would stay and live out the rest of his formative years. He graduated from Woodrow Wilson High School in the year 1947, and his senior yearbook picture housed the quote, "likes math; a future stockbroker."

Even at the age of 6, Buffett was attempting to find ways to flex his entrepreneurial skills. He started selling chewing gum packs full of the popular gum *Juicy Fruit*, one of the first principles he ever employed when it came to business would be the first time he was asked to sell one piece and not the entire pack. He made the decision not to sell under the impression that there would then be an open package of 4 pieces that he might not be able to sell to anyone else individually. This was a smart move on his part; he was beginning to learn the very beginning stages of how professional business institutions operate.

His first ever price markup at 6 years of age? $0.02 profit per pack.

While many people might smile and think this a cute venture for a child, it was the first foundational success Buffett had when it came to the entrepreneurial marketplace. He soon progressed, using his profits to purchase six packs of *Coca-Cola* sodas for $0.25 from his own grandfather's grocery store, entitled *Buffett and Son*. He would then turn around and sell each individual Coke can for $0.05 a piece. His first expansion in the business world.

The profit from that venture? $0.05 per pack.

Notice that, even for a six-year-old, this is an increase in profit. But, his young and vibrant financial spirit did not stop there.

At the young age of 11, Buffett purchased his first ever stock. He saved his money from his local entrepreneurial adventures and purchased six shares of what is now known as CITGO, the oil company. At the time, they were being sold for $38 per share, and he purchased three for himself and gave the other three to his sister, Doris Buffett.

At the time, that was all the money he had accrued from his entrepreneurial adventures as a child. While he might not have practiced the age-old concept of portfolio diversification, he did continue to do that throughout the entity of his investment career. I mean, we cannot expect children to be perfect!

While he owned those six shares, the stock price ended up falling to $27. But, he did not cave into the traditional knee-jerk reaction of selling, and it paid off. The stock soon skyrocketed to over $40 a share, and he would end up selling the stock at that price. A success but also a learnable moment, the stock would end up shooting to over $200 a piece just a short time later.

Buffett considered this his first lesson in how the stock market worked, internalizing each one along the way. This was the first ever stock market venture of the man who would come to be known as the Bible-authoring investor for future generations of investors to come.

When Buffett was 13, he got a taste of the tax life. He filed his first-ever tax return, and on that return he deducted his bike as a work expense for $35. Even at the age of 13, he understood what was necessary in filing taxes and what he could do as a self-employed entrepreneur in order to lower his taxable income, which is absolutely astounding. Many grown adults do not understand this concept. However, it gets better: when Buffett was 15 years old, he would end up making $175 a month selling the Washington Post hard copy newspapers, and this is when he would get his lesson in savings. He ended up saving over $1,200 from this job alone, and he eventually drew upon his savings so he could purchase a 40-acre piece of Farmland in his hometown of Omaha.

Yes, $1,200 to buy 40 acres of land in Nebraska.

Just before he graduated high school at 18, Buffett and his friend, Donald Danly, began a company called *Wilson Coin Operated Machines.* This was a business that would purchase various pinball machines for $25 and put them in nearby shops, such as barbershops. *Wilson Coin* would end up profiting both of the boys to the tune of $50 per week each. This business would also be his first experience in selling his own company, eventually selling for $1200 to a war veteran. Buffett saw an enormous amount of success in his flourishing teenage years. In fact, it is for that reason he decided to skip

—

college and go directly into business. However, this emotional decision was wholly overruled by his father, and Buffett would end up attending the Wharton School at the University of Pennsylvania. The pressure from his father might have deterred him from an automatic business path, but it would lead him to a great deal of success in the nearby future. This is where the influence of Benjamin Graham would first appear, and during his college tenure he would transfer from the University of Pennsylvania to the University of Nebraska at Lincoln.

He graduated with a Bachelor of Science in Business Administration at the incredibly young age of 19, and he would then enroll into the Columbia Business School at Columbia University in order to pursue his Master's of Science in Economics. One thing that pushed him towards this university for graduate studies is the fact that he was rejected by Harvard Business School. However, this would prove to be one of the best things that ever happened to him, Benjamin Graham worked and taught at the Columbia Business School he was going to be attending.

The business beginnings of Warren Buffett may bring smiles to our faces when we think about the childlike innocence of selling chewing gum and hard copy newspapers. What we do not realize, however, was the imperative foundation being laid in the formative cornerstone years of that young six year old's mind. Even in his teenage years, Buffett was a mathematical force to be reckoned with, something he put to good use, by the time he graduated college at 19 years of age he had almost $10,000 in savings.

Although his financial achievements were impressive as a youngster, as to be expected it was only after college Buffet started to really flourish.

Lessons Learned:

- You're never too young to start.
- Experience is the best teacher.
- Saving is an important skill to acquire.
- Initial setbacks, (being rejected from Harvard Business School) can sometimes be a blessing in disguise. (going on to be mentored by Benjamin Graham at Columbia Business School)

Beginnings in Business

"The business schools reward difficult complex behavior more than simple behavior, but simple behavior is more effective."

Buffett's business ventures out of college set the tone for what Buffett would be doing for the rest of his life. From 1951 to 1954 he worked with Buffett-Falk & Co. as a premier investment salesman, and then jumped ship to Graham-Newman Corp. in 1954, where he would work for two years as a security analyst. Then, he would find himself at Buffett Partnership, Ltd. as a general partner until 1969, and then by 1970 he would become Chairman and CEO of Berkshire Hathaway Inc.

Just after Buffett graduated college, his personal savings had grown to $9,800.00, and he intended to make sure that money was put to good use. In the following years he wanted to make sure he made as many connections as possible that would not only be to his benefit, but could also help establish long-term friendships that he could enjoy throughout the career he had planned.

Buffett had an incredible amount of determination when he was younger. In April 1952, Buffett ended up discovering that his biggest influence, Benjamin Graham, was actually on the board of GEICO insurance at the time. He understood that a chance not taken was one he would always regret, so at the spur of the moment, he booked himself a train trip out to his hometown of Washington, D.C. in order to knock on the door of GEICO headquarters. After knocking for well over half an hour, a janitor finally allowed him entrance, and he ended up talking himself into a meeting with GEICO's Vice President, Lorimer Davidson. The two ended up talking about the insurance business well throughout the day, forging what would become a life-long friendship in the process.

Davidson has stated on various occasions that he knew Buffett to be an extraordinary individual after only speaking with him for 15 minutes. It was at this point in Buffett's life he still desperately wanted to pursue a career on Wall Street. But, not only was his father vehemently against it, his lifelong influence, Graham, was as well. In response, Buffett offered to work for Graham, even stating he would do it free of charge. Graham ultimately refused, and many consider this the worst move Graham has ever made.

After being downtrodden by his father and refused by his mentor, Buffett went back to Omaha and began working as a stockbroker whilst also taking a public speaking course by the famous author Dale Carnegie. Public speaking was a big fear of Buffet's and he credits taking this course and overcoming his fear as one of the key pillars to his success. The ability to communicate effectively to groups of people is an essential skill for any leader to possess. He utilized what he learned in Carnegie's class and filtered it into teaching his own "Investment Principles" class. This class was scheduled as a night course at the University of Nebraska at Omaha, and he found that the average age of his students was way more than twice his own.

This brings us to Buffett's first major loss: his side investment into a Sinclair Texaco gas station. He simply could not turn a profit on this particular gas station, and it ended up going under along with the money he had invested into the place. But, Buffett would finally get a chance to work with his mentor in 1954. He accepted a job at Benjamin Graham's partnership with a starting salary of $12,000.00 a year. He found Graham to be an incredibly tough boss, and he found himself clashing with decisions Graham was making within the stock market. Graham's base principle was that stocks provided a very wide margin of safety after weighing specific tradeoffs between their face price and their intrinsic value. Buffett has adamantly preached that this made sense to him at the time, but has admitted to wondering if this strict weighing scale of stocks caused the company to miss out on big opportunities to cash in with winners that others had found appealing even though they did not pass Graham's standards. Having already married and had his first child with his wife, Buffett was feeling the pressure to succeed in the life he had chosen. Fortunately, he had kept up his good habit of saving that he developed in childhood.

When Benjamin Graham retired in 1956 and closed his partnership, Buffett's personal savings had reached well over $170,000.00. In today's day and age, that would be around $1.5 million. Having experienced the birth of his second child with the love of his life, he found himself grateful for the savings he had accrued, because when the partnership closed he took that money and began Buffett Partnership Ltd. He ended up investing $100,000.00 of his own money, part of which came from what he saved in college, and he got other friends and family members to invest a total of $105,000.00 into this new venture of his.

By the time 1957 came around, Buffett was operating three different partnerships. Soon after that his third child was born, and he found himself expanding his partnerships that he worked with to five by the end of that year. It seemed that, whenever a child came along, Buffett dug his heels into the ground even. Then, just shy of 1960, his company grew to six separate partnerships, where he would eventually meet his future business partner, Charlie Munger. He would end up forging such a strong relationship with Munger that he would eventually make Munger Vice Chairman of Berkshire Hathaway.

The young business mogul had his hands full from the very beginning: from being turned down by his mentor to work for free all the way to experiencing his first true loss in the Sinclair Texaco gas station, Buffett could have easily thrown in the towel and found another profession. But, he didn't. Instead, he knuckled down, utilized the birth of his children as massive influencers for his emotional energy, and kept on doing what he knew he could do best.

In the end, this young business mogul grew to be one of the wealthiest individuals in the world.

Lessons learned:

- Buffett experienced his first great loss in the investment community when he was in his latter 20s – even the best fail.
- Buffett credits the ability to speak in public essential to business.
- His lessons in savings served him well and allowed him to start Buffett Partnership, Ltd.
- Finding a good mentor is important.

The Young Business Mogul

"There are 309 million people out there that are trying to improve their lot in life. And we've got a system that allows them to do it."

By the age of 27, Buffett had acquired more partnerships than anyone else his age, managing five different partnerships all from the inside of his own home. What was incredible was that at the ripe age of 28, after 3 years of working with these partnerships, Buffett had ended up doubling his own partners' monies. Every single person that had become a partner underneath Buffett Partnerships, LTD. had seen a massive gain in profit. He made a promise to his partners when they took a risk on him that he would be able to make them the money they deserved.

He stayed true to that promise.

At the age of 29, Buffett was introduced to Charlie Munger, who would later become the Vice Chairman of Berkshire Hathaway. They became great friends and developed a wonderful business relationship. Munger would be by his side as Buffett reached many important milestones in his young career. At the age of 31, Buffett was running several different partnerships outside his home, and these partnerships were worth a few million dollars. Buffett himself ended up making his first million-dollar investment in Dempster, which was a windmill manufacturing company. However, every budding business entrepreneur investment has that one account that makes up the bulk of their portfolio, and for Buffett, at the time, that company was Sanborn Map Company. They accounted for 35% of the partnership's assets.

Sanborn was selling at $45 a share when the overall value of its investment portfolio was being valued at $65 a share. This meant the company's shares were drastically undervalued by $20, and Buffett told Sanborn Map Company that he could make up that $20 a share difference. He ended up on the board.

In 1962, Buffett ended up traveling to New York to meet old friends in order to acquire more partners and raise more capital. He ended up putting a few hundred thousand dollars in his pocket from that trip while selling to them that, at the time, Buffett Partnerships was worth $7.2 million. After acquiring these partnerships, Buffett took a step back to look at the success he had achieved, and he ended up making the smart move of merging all of his Partnerships into one umbrella.

The rename? Buffett Partnership LTD.

During the time of this partnership merger, a few things happened that would change the course of his career forever: Charlie Munger, Buffett's best friend by this point, introduced him to the CEO of Dempster, Harry Bottle. Buffett watched Bottle cut costs to Dempster, lay off workers, and ended up helping Dempster generate a lot of upfront cash. Buffett witnessed this turnaround, was impressed by it, invested in it, and was also able to learn from Bottle's actions. However, around the same time, Buffett noticed that Berkshire Hathaway was selling their stock for only $8 a share. He saw the value in that company even though no one else did, and started buying them up aggressively

This would turn out to be the wisest move of his career. Buffett was determined to turn a profit off Dempster and everything that Bottle had done to rejuvenate it, so when Buffett saw the opportunity, he sold Dempster for a $2.3 million gain, which was three times his original invested amount. During this time, Buffett was also aggressively purchasing Berkshire Hathaway stocks, even though they had gone from $8 a share to $14 a share. Because of this, after his aggressive buying venture, Buffett Partnership LTD. became the single largest shareholder of Berkshire Hathaway.

At this point, Buffett was known to have incredible business-savvy knowledge when it came to recognizing potentially worthwhile investments. For example, in 1964, American Express fell victim to the salad oil scandal. This particular scandal involved Allied Crude Vegetable Oil in New Jersey, and was based around the fact that the owner of this company, Anthony De Angelis, realized he could secure specific loans based on the company's inventory of salad oil. So, he started fudging the numbers: he was making it look as if ship-loads of salad oil were arriving at his docks, fooling inspectors who would confirm the ships were full of oil thus allowing the company to obtain millions of dollars in loans. The reality of the situation was that most of these ships were filled with water, and only the few top feet were covered in salad oil in order to give the appearance that the entire ship had salad oil on it. Since the oil was floating on top of the water, it appeared to the inspectors that the ships were, in fact, loaded with oil. The company even went so far as to transfer different amounts of oil between different tanks while entertaining these inspectors at lunch in order to keep them fooled.

All in all, Allied ended up claiming to have 1.8 billion pounds of salad oil when, in reality, they only had 110 million.

Why is this such a scandal? Because the claimed inventory was the basis for the entire company raising $180 million from investors. The faked numbers fooled the investors into thinking the company was much lucrative than it was, and they ended up investing in a company at an inflated rate of production and value than it was really worth.

That is fraud at its basic foundation.

Naturally, once the scandal was exposed, everyone who had invested in American Express cashed out, which plummeted their stocks. Buffett seized the opportunity and bought 5% of the company stocks when their shares fell to a mere $35 a share, turning him a massive profit later.

However, his tenure with Berkshire Hathaway was far from over. By the age of 35, Buffett had $4 million he invested into Walt Disney after meeting with the man himself, which amounted to 5% of the company at the time. After this deal with an incredibly prominent individual in the entertainment industry, Buffett was well on his way to becoming one of the largest business figures of his generation. His luck and business-savvy experience did not stop there: around this same time, Buffett ended up taking complete control of Berkshire Hathaway. During his control, he named Ken Chace the CEO of the company. That appointment sealed his fate, with his name always being synonymous with the company.

Buffett saw so much success in the first few years of his business career that in 1966 he closed his partnership to new money. Buffett ended up writing in a personal letter that unless it appeared to him that particular circumstances were going to change, or unless new partners could bring in some sort of asset to the partnership than simply capital, he intended to take on no more partners to Buffett Partnership LTD.

But, that did not stop him from investing. During this same year, Buffett invested in Hochschild, Kohn, which was prominent department store in Baltimore. At this point in time, Buffett's personal investment into the partnership was around $6 million, and he made sure to utilize it wisely. During his tenure at Berkshire Hathaway, Buffett Partnership ended up owning just shy of 60% of the company. At the time, their dividend was $0.10, and it ended up being the first and only dividend the company had ever paid and ever would pay. The partnership, in and of itself, was worth $65 million at this point, and Buffett's personal investment had skyrocketed to $10 million. Buffett ended up holding his investments for a while, even though the current market was a raging bull, stating he was unable to find good investments that would turn a decent profit for him.

It was because of this lack of good investment opportunities that he considered briefly leaving the investment world to pursue other particular interests of his.

But, do not forget about American Express. The company ended up recouping itself just like Buffett thought it would, and their shares rose to a whopping $180 a share. This ended up making Buffett a $20 million profit on a $13 million investment.

What many have to understand about Warren Buffett is that, for him, there were no mantras to chant. There were no specific rules of the game, there were very few "how-to" outlined books, and there were no online blogs to coach him on how to make good deals. The deals that Buffett made set the stage for all of the outlined "how-to" books, blog posts, and guest lectures given on how to make sound and solid investment deals. Buffett invented the difference between investing in damaged stock and investing in a damaged company, and it made him millions.

Despite all of this, when people think of Warren Buffett they think of two things: Buffett Partnerships LTD. and Berkshire Hathaway.

So, it is time to shine a light on his involvement at Berkshire Hathaway.

Lessons Learned:

- Warren Buffett set the standard for investing in damaged stock versus investing in a damaged company.
- Patience is important when playing the market.
- Eventually, he would take on no more partnerships in Buffett Partnerships LTD. because his outside investments would keep him busier than ever.

The First Company

"If you get into a lousy business, get out of it."

The textile-manufacturing firm, Berkshire Hathaway, was invested into by Buffett in the mid-1960s. Eventually, his investing would take control of the company, and he would find himself firing the owner Seabury Stanton, whom he started purchasing the shares from in the first place. The shares began at $7.60 a share, and by the time he was done investing, the shares were at $14.86. He wanted to purchase stock in the beginning because he saw the trend in their stock prices every time they closed a mill, but he would end up purchasing company control because of an emotionally charged situation. What started as something that piqued his interest turned into an emotionally fueled decision that he would have to subsequently dig his way out of.

At the infamous board meeting where he took control of Berkshire Hathaway, he named Ken Chace the new president and runner of the company with a smile on his face. It is interesting that the company most synonymous with Buffett's name is considered, in his eyes, a great failure. But, this "failure" is what would push Buffett into the insurance sector as well as other investment areas. He would end up taking this failed company with him, making it one of the biggest holding companies the world has ever seen.

When he made this move into the insurance sector in 1985, he was also in the process of closing the last of the textile mills that had been the core business of Berkshire Hathaway. He was still of the mindset that he would sell off the equipment in an attempt to recoup what he felt he had lost, and it is this decision (along with his own personal feelings) that resulted in him closing his namesake partnership to new money. Buffett felt his intelligence in the investment community had been compromised, and he did not want to subject anyone else to the possible investment failures that were coming as a result of his flawed outlooks and logic.

In a letter to his partners, he announced he would be making his first investment into a private business, which was the privately-owned Baltimore department store we mentioned earlier. Buffett was becoming desperate and trying to milk everything around him for what it was worth in order to recoup some sort of monetary gain for his partners. This worked with 1969 showing itself to be the most successful financial year for the partnership. Buffett liquidated the partnership and transferred all the assets to his partners, fulfilling the promise he made to himself.

This is not the whole story of Berkshire Hathaway. After noticing the pattern and the price of its stock whenever the company closed a mill, Buffett began purchasing the stock. During his purchasing endeavors, Buffett realized the textile business was waning and admitted the company's financial situation was not going to improve. So, oral offers were made in order to sell off the remaining parts of the stock that were scattered among the fired employees. Stanton, the current owner of Berkshire Hathaway, ended up attempting to undercut Buffett in the price of the overall stock after orally agreeing to a particular price, making Buffett angry. So angry in fact, that he decided to purchase more of the stock in order to take the controlling interest of the company.

The firing of Stanton was essentially revenge for attempting to undercut the previously agreed upon financial offers.

Now, Buffett was the majority owner of a textile business that was failing. So, what did he do? He slowly took Berkshire Hathaway from a textile industry-based company to a holding company. While the core of Berkshire's business was textiles, he expanded it, as well as his own expertise, into the insurance industry. From there, other investments blossomed whilst he was shutting down Berkshire's mills. He saw the shell of the company as a great way to hold the outstanding stock he was purchasing. Slowly he began utilizing Berkshire as a filtering and holding company for his own convenience and migrated it away from being an actual company within an industry.

Essentially, he slowly made Berkshire Hathaway into a company that held on to other companies outstanding stock. To date, the multinational holding company has its headquarters in Omaha, Nebraska, and completely owns GEICO, Dairy Queen, Fruit of the Loom, Helzberg Diamonds, Pampered Chef, BNSF Railway, and Lubrizol. It also owns an undisclosed percentage of Mars, Incorporated, over 43% of the Kraft Heinz Company, and has significant minority stock holdings in the Coca-Cola Company, IBM, Wells Fargo, Apple, and American Express.

For those of you who are familiar with the stock market, Berkshire Hathaway Inc. is also one of the companies on the S&P 500 Index.

Not bad for a failing textile business.

Berkshire Hathaway is arguably one of his most incredible successes. Even though he consistently states that he could have had a great deal more money had he not invested in Berkshire Hathaway in the first place, no one can deny the utter transformation that took place under Buffett's leadership. Buffett understood the textile industry was failing, and even as he began shutting down mills he utilized the company's name to hold cheap, outstanding stock from other companies he was investing in. With the investment and monetary knowledge he gained in his younger days, he took Berkshire Hathaway from a failing textile mill industry and turned it into one of the biggest conglomerate multinational holding companies the stock market has ever seen.

However, even though Buffett considers Berkshire Hathaway a semi-failure, many people believe he has made bigger mistakes along the way that have resorted in not only lost funds, but lost opportunities. Men like Warren Buffett are not without their failures, and it is those failures they learn from the most.

After all, you do not get to where Warren Buffett is today based on raw knowledge.

Lessons Learned:

- Just like Buffett showed us with the investment he made into Berkshire Hathaway, emotionally charged investments are not always the best investments to make.
- However, just like Buffett also showed us with Berkshire Hathaway, you can then take that bad investment and turn it into something lucrative if you utilize the knowledge you have and apply it.
- Thinking outside the box will only be advantageous if you already know the system.
- Failure is never final.

The First Of Many Failures

"Never get too hung up on mistakes"

Even though we know that Warren Buffett considers Berkshire Hathaway a mistake, there are also many other mistakes the professional investor and business magnate has admitted to. Although Buffett kept Berkshire Hathaway open as a holding company, he still admits to some bad investments he made in the company's name. By the time the end of 2012 rolled around, the infamous holding company owned more than 400 million shares of stock in the U.K. grocery store Tesco. The purchase price was worth over $2 billion, and by the end of 2013, Berkshire Hathaway ended up selling more than 100 million shares that it held of the company.

Why is this bad? In 2014 the share price of the grocery chain tumbled almost 50% when it was revealed the organization was manipulating its profits to the public. The original sale of the stock was based on concerns Buffett had before this revelation, and it was a move that had been very profitable. $43 million, to be exact. But, he would end up not moving fast enough on the remaining 300 million shares after the scandal went public. He admitted in an open letter to his partners that the dawdling he did on selling the remaining shares cost the company over $400 million in after-tax losses.

In 1993, he purchased Dexter Shoe Company for over $400 million in Berkshire Hathaway's stock. He thought the brand had a very competitive advantage, but he watched it fade a few years after his initial investment. He admitted in an open letter to his partners that he cost his investors $3.5 billion, and to this very day the shoe company is the worst monetary deal Buffett has ever made.

Yet another mistake Buffett admits to is taking on debt from Energy Future Holdings. In a 2013 open letter to his shareholders, Buffett stated he wished he had never heard of Energy Future Holdings. Why? When the company was originally formed in 2007, it was supposed to put into motion a large leveraged buyout of electric utility assets based all around the state of Texas. In other words, it was supposed to prevent a monopoly. All of the equity owners within the company put up about $8 billion, and then ended up borrowing a great deal more to complete the deal. Buffett admits that about $2 billion of the debt was purchased by Berkshire, and that it was a decision he made without consulting Charlie Munger. He said, in retrospect, that had he consulted Munger on the decision, Munger would have shot it down and saved him a great deal of money and headache. Buffett ended up predicting that Energy Future Holdings would file for bankruptcy, and that is exactly what happened. Berkshire Hathaway sold their holdings of the company for $260 million just before the company filed for bankruptcy in 2014. All in all, Buffett admitted that the firm suffered $873 million worth of pre-tax loss.

Not all of his regrets came from what he bought and lost. Some of his regrets are from what he did not buy. Within his failure portfolio, not purchasing the Dallas-Fort Worth NBC station was a massive loss to him. At the time, he had a chance to purchase the station for a mere $35 million dollars. In an open letter to his shareholders in 2007, he explained he passed up the chance to purchase the station around the time he purchased Sea's Candies. He admitted to wholeheartedly turning down the offer even though he trusted the person who ran the station alongside having a gut feeling of the incredible growth potential the television station had.

He jokes that the only reason he said "no" was the fact that his mind had gone on vacation and had forgotten to notify him that it was no longer available. He reminisces quite a bit on the missed opportunity, and admits the station could have earned him over $70 million pre-tax in 2016 when the station was valued at over $800 million.

Yet another strike against his portfolio is issuing extra shares of his Berkshire Hathaway stock in order to purchase General Reinsurance. The 1998 purchase is one of the most public deals Warren Buffett has made, and while he has turned it around in recent years, he still has his regrets about purchasing the company. Apparently, the company had some early problems, and in an open letter to his shareholders in 2016, he states that it was a massive mistake on his part to issue over 270,000 shares of Berkshire stock in order to purchase the company. Why? Because that issuance of stock ended up increasing the outstanding shares the company had by over 20%.

In other words, his error caused many Berkshire shareholders to give more money than they received. Some of the reasons for the hit included overlooking the possibility of terrorist attacks (who could have predicted that?) and underwriting the company's losses. Apparently, General Reinsurance did not have enough money in their financial reserves to pay for losses from their old policies, and Berkshire Hathaway would end up taking an $800 million hit from the lack of these reserves.

Buffett also passed upon the opportunity to purchase stock in

Amazon when its IPO first came to light. He admits to admiring the company when it was first started, but that he simply did not understand the power of the model they were working with, also stating that the price of the stock he was offered reflected the power of the model made and not what the company was worth at the time.

He has admitted time and time again that he consistently shies away from investments he does not understand, and while this can be a tried-and-true practice, in this particular instance it bit him in the butt, so to speak. Whilst hindsight is a nice thing to have, the success he could have had would have been huge. When Amazon first issued their IPO, it was at $18 per share in May 1997. As of April 2017, the stock is now valued at a whopping $907 per share.

That is 50 times its initial purchase price.

It can re-assuring to hear the greatest investor of all time making so many mistakes, re-assuring us he is human after all. Whether it is the stock market or any other endeavor in life, it is unrealistic to expect to come out on top every time. Yet another failure that Buffett admits to is the large purchase of ConocoPhillips stock he made. This was yet another move he made without consulting his partner, Charlie Munger, purchasing the stock when gas and oil prices were near their peak. He did not anticipate the massive fall in energy prices that would occur in the last half of the year, and while he admitted that he believed the price of oil would rise in years to come, he also acknowledged it was not happening anytime soon. He attributed his decision to poor timing, and it cost the firm several billion dollars.

All of this information was delivered in an open letter in 2008, and at the time, Berkshire Hathaway owned almost 85 million shares of ConocoPhillips stock. Buffett admitted to spending over $7 billion on the purchase, but when he sold it at market value it only garnered him about $4.4 billion.

Next was Buffett's venture into the Lubrizol Corporation. While Berkshire Hathaway still owns stock in Lubrizol Corp., Buffett's failure to dig deeper about the stock in the first place cost them a great deal in the early stages. In 2011, both Berkshire Hathaway and Buffett came under fire when it was revealed that the chairman of Lubrizol Corp., David Sokol, accused Buffett of a potential takeover. The issue? Sokol had recently purchased a massive amount of stock in the chemicals company, which created a conflict of interest Buffett was not aware of.

Shortly after this accusation was made, Berkshire Hathaway agreed to purchase Lubrizol all together for about $9 billion, which would earn Sokol a $3 million profit. Sokol had not disclosed his recent purchase of Lubrizol shares, and this directly violates insider-trading rules.

While Buffett admits that Sokol mentioned the purchase in passing, Buffett says he failed to ask him about the date of the purchase or the extent of his holdings within the company stock. When Buffett realized his mistake and owned up to it immediately. At a 2011 Berkshire Hathaway meeting, he took the brunt of the blame for the decision.

The last failure we are going to mention is Buffett's admission to purchasing US Airways stock. While this is not technically considered a "Warren Buffett failure," he does have regret over getting involved with the airline industry in the first place. Back in 1989, he purchased over $350 million worth of shares in the airline that has now since been consolidated. The shares never really appreciated in their value, and Forbes even reported that Buffett likely got all of his principal and dividends back. He did not actually lose money on the deal, but Buffett has been incredibly vocal about what he considers to have been the poor investment decision within this purchase.

So, how exactly is this a failure? He stated in a 1997 open letter to his shareholders that the resuscitation that breathed life back into US Airways bordered on simply miraculous. But, while the stock did not appreciate, he also realized it was not going to garner him any type of monetary gain. So, he ended up attempting to unload the Berkshire Hathaway holdings of the company's stock at $0.50 on the dollar per share. While it did not cost him a great deal of money upfront because of a lot of the work the CEO did in order to revive US Airways, it also did not make him a substantial amount of money either. And, in Buffett's mind, that is just as much of a failure as losing money.

With an investment career like Buffett's, your wins need to be more substantial than your losses. The great thing about Buffett's losses is that we can learn a great deal from them. After all, failure is a wonderful teacher of what it isn't always possible to know at the beginning, and if you can take those lessons and continue to apply them like Buffett has throughout his entire career, you can not only save yourself from future losses, you can also potentially give yourself maximum gains in the process. Attempting to avoid all failure will undoubtedly result in failure itself. Learn from these failures and your victories will soon pile up.

Lessons Learned:

- A company is at its peak if it has a viable competitive advantage. If there is nothing that makes it unique, people will not purchase.
- Consult someone on the big moves before diving into an opportunity.
- When an opportunity is presented to you and all of the flags are waving green, take it.
- Always double-check the numbers.
- When consulting someone on massive decisions, make sure they counter you in some way. After all, consulting someone who is similar to you is like consulting yourself, and that is not recommended.
- Don't be too trusting and always ask questions.
- Research fully every single decision and/or investment you make.
- Once the prior research is done, make decisions promptly. If you understand an investment is not right, get out.

The Turning Point

"Tell me who your heroes are and I'll tell you who you'll turn out to be."

Motivational speaker Jim Rohn has said on multiple occasions that every person is a solid average of the five people they spend the most time with. It sheds a great deal of light on how each individual is conditioned and what they are motivated by. It also lends a great deal of perspective to those who surround themselves with bad influences. When it comes to Warren Buffett's opinion, he stated very clearly in his new documentary, *Becoming Warren Buffett*, that the two biggest turning points in his life were when he came out of his mother's womb and when he met Susie. Susie, by the way, is Buffett's first wife who passed away in 2004.

He has stated on numerous occasions that what happened to him would not have happened without her. He constantly mentions her as his rock, his inspiration, and his safe place to fall whenever he made decisions that were not in the best interest of himself and his shareholders. In fact, Buffett states in the documentary that the biggest decision *anyone* will ever make in their lives are who they ultimately choose to marry. A recent conversation between Warren Buffett and Bill Gates at Columbia University brings about a wonderful quote from the man himself that is very opportunistic in this setting: he stated, "you want to associate with people who are the kind of person you'd like to be. You will move in that direction if you do." This is why, to Buffett, the person you marry is one of the most important decisions of your life. Ultimately, they will have the most influence on you in the long term, and that includes your career trajectory.

But, do not take their word for it. A study done in St. Louis by Brittany Solomon and Joshua Jackson at Washington University has shown us that having a conscientious spouse who is involved in the career of their other spouse can boost one's salary significantly. Why? Because "conscientiousness" means taking the time to involve oneself in the activities that help the other to flourish. This attentiveness and generosity comes off to an individual as support, and I am pretty sure everyone currently reading this book understands how gravely important support is in one's life goals. This study even showed us that people who have extremely conscientious spouses, for example, asking their other half about how things are going with their boss, their co-workers, and even inquiring regularly as to one's long-term goals for their career, were shown to be 60% more likely to become promoted within their workplace. This conscientiousness between spouses does not just morph into support, it morphs into planning and flourishing long-term goals.

When Buffett talks about the turning point in his career, the people surrounding him are often mentioned. From the outside we can only speculate. Various opinions mention they believe that turning point to be the moment when he purchased his first ever stock at 11 years old. Many scientists say those formative years, and what you do and experience with them will provide the direction for the rest of your life. However, there are other people that believe that the turning point in Warren Buffett's career was the first $100,000 he made simply investing in stocks. Before he became the massive business magnate he is today, Buffett was simply investing in stocks and playing the stock market as any beginner would. Many people argue that him making his first $100,000 in the stock market solidified within him the desire to make it his career.

From 1949 to 1954, at the age where many people are partying at college and exploring all of their options, Buffett was making his first $100,000 via investments in stock. It is difficult to calculate what exactly his annual returns were, but it is very easy to understand that in order to achieve the wealth that he did during the time that he did, he would have had to have compounded his money at an annual rate of no less than 40% a year. In the world of investment, that is incredibly aggressive, and it paid off in the end to solidify the type of investor Buffett would become.

This is consistent with his own statements he has made during lectures over the years. He has told many of the students that come to listen to him that he made 50% a year on his own portfolio before he ever started his partnership after working with Benjamin Graham. He also said those percentage returns started to lower with each decade. As his wealth grew and his knowledge of the stock market flourished, he became less and less aggressive with his portfolios because he was taking on more and more shareholders that were depending on him and the promises he could bring. He was no longer playing with just his own money, but also the money of others.

From the time he first read *The Intelligent Investor* to the time he started his partnership, Buffett invested in Marshall Wells, GEICO, Greif Brother's Cooperage, Philadelphia Reading & Coal, Cleveland Worsted Mills, Western Insurance, National American Fire Insurance, Rockwood Chocolate, and Union Street Railway. He spent a great deal of time working his investments to his advantage, but did see some setbacks with some bad decisions. However, he took those lessons and applied them to future investments, and this would be the culmination of his college career: learning the stock market by participating in it.

Many people put Benjamin Graham and Warren Buffett side-by-side, and it is not surprising as to why they do that: Buffett has stated on several occasions that Benjamin Graham was his inspiration and, in many ways, his mentor. Buffett, before he started taking Graham's classes at Columbia University, read Graham's book *The Intelligent Investor*. At this point in time, Buffett already had stock within Marshall Wells, and with a $200 stock price, within it housed $62 of earnings per share. The stock was selling a little over three times its earnings, which averages to about 30%. He sought Graham's advice as to where he could go from there.

Here is the main difference between Graham and Buffett: Buffett did not invest the way Graham did. It is what caused them to butt heads so much when Buffett was finally working for Graham and the partnership Graham owned. Buffett is a return on investment investor and is obsessed with the idea of compounding, while Graham was a value investor. Simply put, Graham saw value within a stock, and purchased that stock at a massive discount for a safe and guaranteed return. However, Buffett was not merely purchasing cheap stock that had value, he was also gunning for massive returns on the stock he purchased for both himself and his partners. Honestly, *this* feels like the true turning point in Buffett's career. Just because you decide you want to be an investor does not mean you understand the type of investor you wish to be. There are many different types, and not all of them make for good careers. When Warren Buffett finally solidified the type of investor he wanted to be based on the mistakes he saw his mentor make, this is what would re-enforce the type of investment decisions he would make in the coming years. And this is how he would make his current fortune.

Lessons Learned:

- Buffett feels the two turning points in his life were when he was born and when he met his wife, Susie.
- Many others speculate the turning point in his career was when he made his first $100,000 during his college years simply investing in stock.
- The true turning point in his career in my opinion was when he solidified the type of investor he wanted to be, which would influence all of his investment decisions to come for the rest of his life.
- As important as it is to seek out mentors for advice, you should always choose your own path.

15 Success Principles To Live By

People from every age and every industry have been eating up whatever this man has recommended for decades, and rightly so. This is a list of the greatest lessons I believe Warren Buffett has shared with the world. This set of principles covers both life and investing. To become the best you must learn from the best.

Extraordinary Focus

During HBO's new documentary *Becoming Warren Buffett,* there is a scene with one of Buffett's friends, a man you may have heard of – Bill Gates. Whilst sitting together at a table, both men were asked to write on a piece of paper the one thing they felt had contributed most to their success. Sure enough, both men had unknowingly written down the same word: focus. It surely can't be a coincidence that two of the most successful men of this era chose the same answer, only further highlighting the importance of complete focus to achieving great success.

Set a concrete goal

Following on from the above point, in today's age it can be hard to focus with all the distractions modern day life provides. This is where setting a concrete goal is a must. Buffett set himself the goal to have $1 million net worth by the time he was 30. Just setting a large goal isn't enough; he also created a plan on how to achieve that goal. He wrote down each milestone he would need to accomplish along the way and didn't deviate until he had achieved it. Setting up a clear path and plan to follow makes it much easier to focus.

Master the rules of the game

To quote Einstein: "You have to learn the rules of the game. And then you have to play better than anyone else." Although you need to set a goal and focus on it, without educating yourself as to *how* you can make it happen, progress will be slow. You really need to understand whatever system it is you're playing. Still to this day Buffett allocates a significant part of his time to reading and educating himself, more so than actually taking action.

Choose your own path

Once you learn the rules of the game, you can now decide how you want to play it. Buffett sticks to the type of businesses he understands and avoids recent trends and online-based companies altogether. He has made very few investments or trades relative to his extremely long career. He found out what worked for him and stuck at it, undistracted by what others are doing.

Live below your means

Buffett still lives in the same modest home in Omaha, Nebraska. He purchased it for a little over $31,000 in 1958. To this day, he considers it the third best investment he has ever made, behind the rings for his two wives. He also believes in watching the small expenses, once stating his admiration for a friend who only painted the side of the office building that was facing the road.

Keep borrowing to a minimum / Save before spending

The two points go together perfectly. Over such a long career in the investment game, Buffett has never borrowed a significant amount. Initially relying on his savings and then using future profits. He advises to set aside a specific amount of money each month as if it is a bill that must be paid, then once the pot reaches a certain point; invest.

Reinvest profits

It can be tempting to spend all that you earn; this isn't a wise move in the investment game and is sure to slow down progress. Buffett learned this lesson early in life with his pinball machine business. With the profits he made from the first machine, he used to buy more. Eventually he sold the business and used the proceeds to purchase his first stocks. As they say, the rest is history.

Efficiency is key

As mentioned, focus is extremely important, but choosing the correct things to focus on is part of the challenge. If your attention is being pulled all over the place, it is important to realize this and focus on the truly important things. One way Buffett mitigates wasting time is by barely attending any meetings. His now infamous yearly open letters can reach a larger number of people and saves him from having to attend countless meetings, a great tool for time management.

Avoid "thumb-sucking"

Gather whatever information you need to make the decision you are faced with and just decide. Buffett refers to any unnecessary sitting, thinking or procrastinating as "thumb-sucking."

Nail down the deal before you start

Leverage is always at a high before you begin the job, as that is when you are able to offer something the other party wants.

Use this to your advantage and make sure the details are perfectly clear. Buffett learned this one the hard way. As a young kid, his grandfather hired him and a friend to help dig out the family grocery store after a particularly strong blizzard. The two worked for five hours shoveling away until their hands were nearly frozen solid. His grandfather rewarded them with less than 90 cents to share.

Stay persistent

Tenacity and grit over the long term will always beat natural talent and even a more established competitor. When Buffett acquired the Nebraska Furniture Mart in 1983, it was mainly due to how impressed he was with how the founder, Rose Blumkin, did business. Starting as a pawnshop, she built the business into the largest furniture store in America through a combination of persistent grinding and merciless negotiating skills. This allowed her to undersell her biggest rivals, impressing Buffett in the process.

Know when to change tactics

Persistence is one thing, but being self-aware enough to realize when it's time to move on or change tactics is equally as important. In his teen years Buffett visited a racetrack, as so many of us do, he bet on a race and lost. In an effort to recoup his funds, he bet on another, losing again. By this stage he had wasted a week's earnings and felt sick, a mistake he never made again.

Assess risk honestly

When Buffett is assessing risk, he does it with complete honesty. No exaggerations or downplays, after all the easiest person to fool is yourself. When his son Howie was accused of price-fixing by the FBI in 1995, he advised him to imagine the best and worst case scenarios if he decided to stay with the company. Looking at the situation this way allowed his son to easily see that the risks of staying far outweighed the potential gains. He quit the following day.

Be willing to go against the status quo

You don't always have to follow what everybody else is doing. Buffett was initially seen as quite odd when he started managing money from his home in Omaha and not Wall Street. He strung together $105,000 from only a few investors and was expected to fail. Fast-forward 14 years and he was worth $100,000,000.

Understand what success actually means

Despite his vast fortune, Buffett does not measure success in monetary terms. He has no desire for any monuments or buildings to be dedicated in his name and has pledged to give away almost all of his entire fortune. Instead he defines success in a different way to how you might imagine:

"When you get to my age, you'll measure your success in life by how many of the people you want to have love you actually do love you. That's the ultimate test of how you lived your life."

Another skill of note that Buffett describes as essential to his success is the ability to speak in public. Early on in his career, Buffett was petrified of public speaking. He recognized that this skill would be crucial in achieving his goals, so he enrolled himself onto a course that was taught by Dale Carnegie. Today, he always tells those he lectures that the ability to effectively communicate is essential to success in almost any field, but is especially vital in the financial industry. Through incorporating these principles into your life you may not end up as wealthy as Warren Buffett or Bill Gates, but having a sincere focus on what you are trying to accomplish - combined with a perseverance to stick with it day in and day out - will make for an incredibly successful you.

25 Life-Changing Quotes

"Rule No.1: Never lose money. Rule No.2: Never forget rule No.1."

This is the golden rule according to Buffett and is pretty self-explanatory. Decisions should be made on a financial basis, not personal.

"Be fearful when others are greedy. Be greedy when others are fearful."

Although a complete oversimplification, the key to investing well is to buy low and sell high. Buffett believes in cautious investing when the market is booming and when the market is down; take advantage on the true value deals that will be on offer. This method has been the basis for his most successful investments.

"The difference between successful people and really successful people is that really successful people say no to almost everything."

As mentioned earlier, Warren Buffett and Bill Gates attribute focus as the number one quality to achieving success. Direct focus is as much about having a not to do list more so than a to-do list. Block out distractions and focus only on the most important.

"I've seen more people fail because of liquor and leverage - leverage being borrowed money. You really don't need leverage in this world much. If you're smart, you're going to make a lot of money without borrowing."

Success can come through various paths but failures usually happen around a few key themes, Buffett notes his common observations towards failure in this quote and it is worth remembering.

"Price is what you pay. Value is what you get."

This quote actually originated from Buffett's mentor Benjamin Graham, but Buffett has used it himself on various occasions. This distinction between value and price is important to fully grasp and is one that many struggle with. Price is the objective or market value of the stock. Value or "What you get," is in simplest form the discounted present value of future cash flows.

"It takes 20 years to build a reputation and five minutes to ruin it. If you think about that, you'll do things differently."

Being mindful when making decisions is essential. Your reputation may not reflect the person you actually are, but it is how others will perceive you. For someone like Buffett who is the head of a multi-billion dollar corporation, reputation is key to developing trust.

"Someone is sitting in the shade today because someone planted a tree a long time ago."

Buffett believes in long term investing. When purchasing a company he often has the intent of holding onto it for at least ten years, as that's where the most accurate trends can be seen. Investing in his eyes, is a lifelong journey and not a get rich quick scheme.

"It's far better to buy a wonderful company at a fair price than a fair company at a wonderful price."

Buffett invests with value in mind and not price. A strong company with strong leaders will do most of the work for him. Bargains aren't always worth the money due to the extra hassle they can bring.

"Risk comes from not knowing what you're doing."

There may be an element of risk over the short term with stocks, but it is no accident the same people do well year after year over the long term. Even though chance is involved, Buffett knows over time skill will win out over luck.

"Over a period of time there are going to be good and bad years, there is nothing to be gained by getting enthused or depressed about the sequence in which they occur."

As you should invest with the long term in mind, you should also judge your results in the same way. Outperforming the market is a more accurate indicator of heading in the right direction, even if your numbers are neutral or negative.

"We've long felt that the only value of stock forecasters is to make fortune tellers look good. Even now, Charlie and I continue to believe that short-term market forecasts are poison and should be kept locked up in a safe place, away from children and also from grown-ups who behave in the market like children."

As to why you should avoid short term results and forecasts, see above. In basic terms Buffett believes short-term forecasts to be both unreliable and unnecessary as they focus investors on the short-term, something Buffett disagrees strongly against.

"It's better to hang out with people better than you. Pick out associates whose behavior is better than yours and you'll drift in that direction."

The old saying by Jim Rohn stands true: "You are the average of the five people you spend most time with."

"It's only when the tide goes out that you discover who's been swimming naked."

This quote came from a letter Buffett wrote to his shareholders in 2001; he is referencing those who take big risks that they can't back up will eventually be exposed when the market drops.

"You only have to do a very few things right in your life so long as you don't do too many things wrong."

Sticking to what you know

and what you're good at is advice Buffett often gives. Become an expert in your chosen field and the rest will follow.

"I insist on a lot of time being spent, almost every day, to just sit and think. That is very uncommon in American business. I read and think. So I do more reading and thinking, and make less impulse decisions than most people in business. I do it because I like this kind of life."

Think things through properly. It may sound like common sense but in today's fast paced society it is a rarity. All big decisions deserve an allocation of time spent thinking them through, avoiding recklessness when possible.

"The most important thing to do if you find yourself in a hole is to stop digging."

Occasionally, it's best to do nothing at all.

"Should you find yourself in a chronically leaking boat, energy devoted to changing vessels is likely to be more productive than energy devoted to patching leaks."

Following on from the last quote, sometimes it is best to cut your losses and jump ship. Successful people don't call a bet with a losing hand. They recognize when something is sinking and know it's time to get a new boat.

"I try to buy stock in businesses that are so wonderful that an idiot can run them. Because sooner or later, one will."

You can't put your complete faith in people. Even if you associate with the right people, they may still let you down someday.

"Chains of habit are too light to be felt until they are too heavy to be broken."

You are the result of your daily habits. Make sure you cultivate good ones; because the longer you have them the harder they'll be to break.

"You're dealing with a lot of silly people in the marketplace; it's like a great big casino and everyone else is boozing. If you can stick with Pepsi, you should be O.K."

Buffett's lesson here: Curb your enthusiasm. The markets are an exciting place but if you can keep your cool and focus on the long run, you'll be in a much better position. We live our lives day-to-day in the short run; we need to focus our investments for the long run.

"We concentrated on identifying one-foot hurdles that we could step over rather than because we acquired any ability to clear seven-footers."

Buffett keeps his investment methods simple. Instead of investing in businesses that are in a highly regulated industry with plenty of seven foot problems, he chooses the more "straight-forward" businesses that have to deal with common everyday problems. The best way to solve a problem, in his eyes, is to avoid it happening.

"In a bull market, one must avoid the error of the preening duck that quacks boastfully after a torrential rainstorm, thinking that its paddling skills have caused it to rise in the world. A right-thinking duck would instead compare its position after the downpour to that of the other ducks on the pond."

In plain English, Buffett is stating that just because a business does well in a bull market, this doesn't mean it is a good investment for all markets. Buying stock high because you hope to sell it an even higher price isn't wise.

"At Berkshire, we make no attempt to pick the few winners that will emerge from an ocean of unproven enterprises. We're not smart enough to do that, and we know it. Instead, we try to apply Aesop's 2,600-year-old equation to opportunities in which we have reasonable confidence as to how many birds are in the bush and when they will emerge (a formulation that my grandsons would probably update to 'A girl in a convertible is worth five in the phonebook.')."

Keep up with the times but don't go crazy taking unnecessary risks -- that is, risks without adequate or compensating payoffs. Know the risks you are taking in the expectation the payoff will be there at the end more often than not.

"I call investing the greatest business in the world ... because you never have to swing … There's no penalty except opportunity lost. All day you wait for the pitch you like; then when the fielders are asleep, you step up and hit it."

If you are a long-run investor and have no leverage, then you can be very selective in what you can buy. Wait for a good opportunity if you're investing. Trading for the sake of trading is not advisable according to Buffett.

"I always knew I was going to be rich. I don't think I ever doubted it for a minute."

You need to be certain of your success, even when no one else is.

What Is Warren Buffett Doing Now?

"Retirement is not my idea of living."

As of today, Warren Buffett is not only giving various lectures around the world, he is also still doing what he loves to do: investing. According to Berkshire Hathaway's latest SEC filing, Berkshire's stake in Apple quadrupled to around 57 million shares, and Berkshire was revealed to have many investments in several airlines stocks, such as Delta and United Continental. A new stake in Monsanto also came to light, totaling around eight million shares, which is to be valued at over $800 million. The biggest portfolio change to the Berkshire Hathaway holding company has been the 167 million shares they purchased in Sirius XM.

However, Berkshire Hathaway and Warren Buffett have also been selling. While Buffett used to be a 13 million shareholder in Walmart, he recently cut those shares to a mere 1.4 million. No one really knows why, but the assumption is that online retailing and shopping is changing the landscape of brick-and mortar-stores, as well as the future of their stock. Berkshire also sold all of its shares in Verizon, Deere, and Kinder Morgan. While no one has made an official statement on why these have completely fallen off Berkshire Hathaway's portfolio, many state it is because of valuation issues that caused stock to plummet lower than Buffett was comfortable. Want to know what I think? I think we will watch Warren Buffett continue to do exactly what he loves to do until the day he regretfully passes from this planet. The truth of the matter is: when you find a burning passion and desire for something, you will want to do it for the rest of your life. It is one of the many fruitful tips he gives in his infamous lectures, and it is yet another lesson we see played out in his own life.

Long live the Oracle of Omaha.

Thanks for checking out my book. I hope you found this of value and enjoyed it. But before you go, I have one small favor to ask…

Would you take 60 seconds and write a quick blurb about this book on Amazon?

Reviews are the best way for independent authors (like me) to get noticed, sell more books, and it gives me the motivation to continue producing. I also read every review and use the feedback to write future revisions – and even future books. Thanks again.

Printed in Great Britain
by Amazon

24203781R00047